MARRIAGE

GOD'S DESIGN FOR INTIMACY

JAMES & MARTHA REAPSOME

11 STUDIES FOR INDIVIDUALS OR GROUPS

Life
Builder
Study

ivp

INTER-VARSITY PRESS
36 Causton Street, London SW1P 4ST, England
Email: ivp@ivpbooks.com
Website: www.ivpbooks.com

Originally published in the United States of America in the LifeGuide® Bible Studies series in 1986 by InterVarsity Press, Downers Grove, Illinois
Second edition published in 1999
First published in Great Britain in 2018

British Library Cataloguing-in-Publication Data
A catalogue record for this book is available from the British Library.

ISBN: 978–1–78359–694–2

Printed in Great Britain by Ashford Colour Press Ltd, Gosport, Hampshire

Inter-Varsity Press publishes Christian books that are true to the Bible and that communicate the gospel, develop discipleship and strengthen the church for its mission in the world.

IVP originated within the Inter-Varsity Fellowship, now the Universities and Colleges Christian Fellowship, a student movement connecting Christian Unions in universities and colleges throughout Great Britain, and a member movement of the International Fellowship of Evangelical Students. Website: www.uccf.org.uk. That historic association is maintained, and all senior IVP staff and committee members subscribe to the UCCF Basis of Faith.

Contents

Getting the Most Out of *Marriage*

Marriage as an institution is under attack as never before, yet people are not avoiding marriage. Statistics show that divorced persons keep trying again and again to make successful marriages, even two and three times. Marriage counseling as a profession is booming. Books about marriage are gobbled up by eager readers. Despite the wreckage of marriages all around us, marriage will survive. The question is, Can we make marriage all that God intended it to be when he gave it for humanity's happiness and blessing?

A recently widowed woman said, "Even if we had had only two years together, I would have been grateful to have been married to him. He was such a gentle, loving person."

What makes such marriages work? Isn't it the spiritual qualities expressed by two people, qualities that generate currents of deep affection and mutual respect? These spiritual qualities are God's gift to us. They express our new nature in Christ. When we work to develop integrity, purity, wisdom and love, we are becoming more Christlike and less confined by that jumble of things we call our personality. We become better wives and husbands.

These studies are designed to help you understand marriage as God intends it. You will discover the Bible's realistic approach to marriage and the principles God gave for enjoying it fully.

The first seven studies explore God's original and restored design for marriage. Studies eight through ten examine biblical principles for handling common problems in marriage. The final study probes God's definition and description of love.

If you are married, you may find the "Now or Later" sections at the end of each study helpful to work through as a couple between studies. These are intended to help you develop new skills, clarify sources of conflict so they can be resolved and provide opportunity to express appreciation for one another.

May God use these studies to help you "to live in such harmony with one another, in accord with Christ Jesus, that together you may with one voice glorify the God and Father of our Lord Jesus Christ" (Romans 15:5-6 RSV).

Suggestions for Individual Study

1. As you begin each study, pray that God will speak to you through his Word.

2. Read the introduction to the study and respond to the personal reflection question or exercise. This is designed to help you focus on God and on the theme of the study.

3. Each study deals with a particular passage—so that you can delve into the author's meaning in that context. Read and reread the passage to be studied. If you are studying a book, it will be helpful to read through the entire book prior to the first study. The questions are written using the language of the New International Version, so you may wish to use that version of the Bible. The New Revised Standard Version is also recommended.

4. This is an inductive Bible study, designed to help you discover for yourself what Scripture is saying. The study includes three types of questions. *Observation* questions ask about the basic facts: who, what when, where and how. *Interpretation* questions delve into the meaning of the passage. *Application* questions help you discover the implications of the text for growing in Christ. These three keys unlock the treasures of Scripture.

Write your answers to the questions in the spaces provided or in a personal journal. Writing can bring clarity and deeper understanding of yourself and of God's Word.

5. It might be good to have a Bible dictionary handy. Use it to look up any unfamiliar words, names or places.

6. Use the prayer suggestion to guide you in thanking God for what you have learned and to pray about the applications that have come to mind.

7. You may want to go on to the suggestion under "Now or Later," or you may want to use that idea for your next study.

Suggestions for Members of a Group Study

1. Come to the study prepared. Follow the suggestions for individual study mentioned above. You will find that careful preparation will greatly enrich your time spent in group discussion.

2. Be willing to participate in the discussion. The leader of your group will not be lecturing. Instead, he or she will be encouraging the members of the group to discuss what they have learned. The leader will be asking the questions that are found in this guide.

3. Stick to the topic being discussed. Your answers should be based on the verses which are the focus of the discussion and not on outside authorities such as commentaries or speakers. These studies focus on a particular passage of Scripture. Only rarely should you refer to other portions of the Bible. This allows for everyone to participate in in-depth study on equal ground.

4. Be sensitive to the other members of the group. Listen attentively when they describe what they have learned. You may be surprised by their insights! Each question assumes a variety of answers. Many questions do not have "right" answers, particularly questions that aim at meaning or application. Instead the questions push us to explore the passage more thoroughly.

When possible, link what you say to the comments of others. Also, be affirming whenever you can. This will encourage some of the more hesitant members of the group to participate.

5. Be careful not to dominate the discussion. We are sometimes so eager to express our thoughts that we leave too little opportunity for others to respond. By all means participate! But allow others to also.

6. Expect God to teach you through the passage being discussed and through the other members of the group. Pray that you will have an enjoyable and profitable time together, but also that as a result of the study you will find ways that you can take action individually and/or as a group.

7. Remember that anything said in the group is considered confidential and should not be discussed outside the group unless specific permission is given to do so.

8. If you are the group leader, you will find additional suggestions at the back of the guide.

1

God's Design for Marriage

Genesis 1:26—2:25

To build a house we need a design and a blueprint from an architect. We want the design to be both beautiful and comfortable, a house that fulfills our dreams. To build a beautiful, satisfying marriage to fill that house we also need a wise designer's plan.

GROUP DISCUSSION. How would you design the foundation for a satisfying marriage? What essential materials would you use?

PERSONAL REFLECTION. Talk to God about your desire to enjoy marriage as he intended you would. Ask him to help you appreciate marriage as he designed it.

God the master Creator, reveals his design in this section of Genesis. *Read Genesis 1:26—2:17.*

---

1. God created man and woman in his image (1:26). What various male and female characteristics help you understand what "the image of God" is?

2. God declares all he has created is very good (1:31). This includes being male or female. How can God's "very good" help you accept and respect the uniqueness of your gender?

3. What responsibilities and resources did God give to the man and woman (1:26-30; 2:8-9, 15-17)?

4. *Read Genesis 2:18-25.* For the first time God declares something in his creation "not good" (2:18). Put yourself in the man's place. How would the parade of animals intensify your loneliness?

5. What was the man's part and God's part in meeting Adam's need?

6. What tone of voice do you think the man used in his reaction to the woman (2:23)?

7. What marriage principles do you draw from 2:24?

8. God created marriage primarily to meet our need for companionship. But sometimes a child or a parent can thwart that purpose. How can you guard your companionship in the midst of the pressure of family responsibilities?

_____

9. Why was there no shame or self-consciousness between the man and woman (2:25)?

Why do you think that fact is noted here?

_____

10. How has this passage helped you see that God provides for our emotional, physical and spiritual needs in his marriage design?

_____

11. What surprises you, comforts you or disturbs you about God's design?

Pray for a deeper understanding of what the creation account has to say about building a Christian marriage.

Now or Later

Reflect on God's design for exclusive, permanent, oneness and companionship in marriage. Consider the steps you can take now to prepare for or to enjoy his design.

2

God's Design Marred

Genesis 3

Occasionally someone will break into an art museum and slash a painting. All of us feel the pain because a beautiful work of art has been marred.

GROUP DISCUSSION. Recall a childhood experience when you damaged a prized family possession or secretly disobeyed your parents. What mixture of emotions did you feel while you waited to be found out?

PERSONAL REFLECTION. Reflect on how pride or guilt has damaged your relationship with God or another person. What pattern of behavior do you see? Ask God for a fresh appreciation for his grace and eagerness to restore the relationship.

In Genesis 1 and 2 we saw how God designed marriage to meet our physical, emotional and spiritual needs. The man and woman experienced openness and ease in their relationship. But something happened to mar that ideal relationship. In Genesis 3 we see how guilt, fear, pride and blame cause barriers between God and us, as well as a host of marital problems. *Read Genesis 3.*

---

1. Focus on Genesis 3:1-7—scene 1 in this drama. Visualize the setting in which the action occurs. How does it contribute to the story?

What conflicts are going on in this scene?

_____

2. What insinuations does Satan make about God in his conversation with the woman (vv. 1-5)?

_____

3. What choices do the woman and her husband make, and why?

_____

4. What immediate change does sin produce in the man and woman (v. 7)?

_____

5. In the previous chapter "the man and his wife were both naked, and they felt no shame" (v. 25). Now Adam and Eve make coverings for themselves. Consider your own emotions. How does sin cause us to hide, to cover ourselves, to feel shame, to be ill at ease with another?

_____

6. Look at verses 8-13 as scene 2 in this drama. God enters the scene asking questions, but not because he needs information. What is God doing for the man and woman by asking them these questions?

_____

7. In this scene what changes have occurred in Adam and Eve's attitude toward God and toward each other (vv. 10, 12-13)?

8. In what way did they die when they ate the fruit?

---

9. How can fear, self-consciousness or blame affect the quality of our relationship with God?

---

10. Look at verses 14-24—scene 3. How does the description of the husband-wife relationship in verse 16 differ from God's original design in chapter 2?

---

11. What do you learn about God from each of his actions toward Adam and Eve in verses 21-24?

---

12. Adam and Eve's sin had consequences for all of God's creation. But which specific contemporary problems between husbands and wives have their source in our basic rebellion against God?

Pray for the Holy Spirit to protect your marriage from failing spiritually.

Now or Later

Adam and Eve are our representatives. Go back through the story looking for all the points where you can identify with their struggles, choices and altered relationships with God and others.

3

God's Design Restored

One of the most heart-warming scenes ever filmed by news cameras shows hundreds of prisoners streaming from German concentration camps as the end of World War II. Few people have ever savored their freedom as much as those people did. They knew what had happened to thousands of their fellow prisoners at the hands of the Nazis.

GROUP DISCUSSION. Encourage each person to complete the sentence, "True freedom is . . . " Try to reach a consensus on a definition of freedom.

PERSONAL REFLECTION. Thank God for the freedom the Holy Spirit brings to everyone who has repented and trusted the Lord Jesus. Ask God to teach you how to appropriate the Holy Spirit's power to overcome sin and live to please God.

Part of the good news of Jesus Christ is that we can be set free from something far worse than a concentration camp—our old sinful ways of living. We are liberated to live under the control and direction of the Holy Spirit. We are free to enjoy the beautiful oneness of God's original design for us. *Read Galatians 5:13-26.*

1. What attitudes and actions are contrasted in this passage?

_____

2. What two possible uses of freedom can a Christian make (v. 13)?

_____

3. In what ways do you face the temptation in marriage to be self-centered rather than serving your spouse in love?

_____

4. In addition to being selfish, Paul also cites the danger of verbal abuse (v. 15). How might a husband or wife destroy each other by verbal biting and devouring?

_____

5. A husband or wife may work long hours in order to serve the family's physical and material needs. But the other spouse may view this "service" as neglecting time together. How can a husband and wife help each other understand what communicates loving service to them?

_____

6. God promises that we can avoid being controlled by our sinful nature if we make the right choices. What do the choices in verses 16, 18 and 25 look like in daily life?

_____

7. How are these acts of our sinful nature destructive to us personally and to our marriages (vv. 19-21, 22-23)?

---

8. What choices can we make to avoid falling into these sins or to get free from any that control us?

---

9. In contrast to the acts of our sinful nature, how does the fruit of the Spirit express the characteristics of God (vv. 22-23)?

---

10. How have you seen the fruit of the Spirit demonstrated in the lives of husbands and wives you know?

---

11. Paul instructs us positively, to *keep in step with the Spirit* (v. 25) and negatively, to *not become conceited, provoking and envying each other* (v. 26). What family tensions would be relieved by obeying each of these commands?

---

12. God's beautiful design for marriage can be ours today in spite of the damage sin has done. What encouragement and instruction do you find in this passage to help you serve one another in love by the power of the Holy Spirit?

Pray for a fresh, positive, optimistic outlook toward Christian marriage.

Now or Later

Recall some of the choices you made this week. Which were living by your sinful nature and which were serving one another in love?

God promises that if you live by the Spirit, it is possible not to gratify the desires of your sinful nature (v. 16). Consider how being led by the Spirit enabled you to make the right choices. Think about how you could respond differently in the situations where you were unloving.

4

God's Design for Wives

Ephesians 5:21-33

You and your spouse have planned a weekend at the lake. You anticipate sleeping in and then devouring a new novel and a hot dog on the beach at sunset. Your spouse dreams of getting a great tan, learning to water ski and eating dinner at an elegant restaurant. As you become aware of these conflicting desires, you both begin wondering whether your weekend will be a total loss.

GROUP DISCUSSION. Consider the situation described above, the weekend at the lake. What advice would you give this couple as they adjust their plans and try to be considerate of each other?

PERSONAL REFLECTION. Thank God for his wise and loving design for marriage. Confess whatever fears or doubts you may have about his design working today. Ask for openness to learn what you need to learn from this study.

Paul writes that being filled with the Holy Spirit affects our worshiping, our singing and our submitting to one another. Then he instructs wives and husbands in living out God's design. In this study we will look at his basic framework for marriage and his instruction to the wife. In study 5 we will consider instructions to the husband. *Read Ephesians 5:21-33.*

1. What information do you find about the wife's role throughout this passage?

2. Why is the command "submit to one another out of reverence for Christ" (v. 21) the appropriate framework for these instructions to wives and husbands?

3. In what situations have you seen two Christians practicing mutual submission out of reverence for Christ?

4. The wife's submission to her husband is compared with submission to the Lord (vv. 22-24). Think about how a Christian submits to the Lord. What attitudes, emotions or struggles are involved for you to submit to the Lord?

5. Paul assumes that both husband and wife are committed to Jesus Christ as Savior and Lord. What implications does this have for those considering marriage today?

6. How can Christ's dual role as head and Savior (v. 23) encourage us to submit to him?

7. If we yield to Christ's lordship, to what extent are we still free to make choices and to express ourselves?

_____

8. In submitting to her husband, how and why can a wife feel free to express her opinions, fears and feelings?

_____

9. What attitudes toward her husband would help a wife submit to him as she would to Christ?

_____

10. What attitudes and actions in a husband would encourage his wife's trust and respect?

Pray for opportunities to better understand what it means to submit to one another.

Now or Later

Whether you are married or not, look for opportunities for mutual submission this week. Discuss one of them later, state how you felt and why you acted or spoke the way you did.

As a couple, look for examples of a wife's submission to her husband. Compare ideas. Did you both recognize the same behaviors or different ones? What insights does this give you about how your spouse understand your actions?

5

God's Design for Husbands

Ephesians 5:21-33

After watching two of his daughters fall in love, Tevye (the father in *Fiddler on the Roof*) wonders if anything like that ever happened to his wife, Golde. So he asks her, "Do you love me?" She recites the details of how faithfully she has served all of his needs. "But do you love me?" he asks again. His wife looks back over twenty-five years of satisfying marriage and admits, "I suppose I do." That kind of love, which is far deeper then emotional infatuation, has staying power.

GROUP DISCUSSION. Think of a marriage you admire. What impresses you about the ways these couples demonstrate love?

PERSONAL REFLECTION. Thank God for what he has taught you this week about his design for marriage. Reflect on Jesus' sacrificial love for you.

To discover how God sees true love *read Ephesians 5:21-33*.

1. What stands out to you about the husband's responsibilities in God's design for marriage?

2. How would Paul's basic command, stated three different ways (vv. 25, 28, 33), help a man to be a better husband?

How does this compare with your ideas of what a husband should be or do?

_____

3. Christ's love for the church is the example of how to love your wife. Why and how did Christ express his love for the church (vv. 25-27)?

_____

4. How can a husband follow Christ's example in his motives and actions with his wife?

_____

5. A husband is to love his wife as his own body (v. 28). In what ways do you love and care for your body?

_____

6. How can a husband follow Jesus' example to "nourish and cherish" (v. 29 RSV) his wife as Christ does his body, the church?

_____

7. The thought of Christ's union with his body prompts Paul to quote God's original design from Genesis 2:24. What new depth of meaning does Paul find in the marriage union?

8. In verse 33 Paul summarizes the basic instruction to husbands and wives. Why are these commands to love and respect unconditional?

———————————————————————————

9. Why does the Bible emphasize responsibilities rather than privileges?

———————————————————————————

10. Look back to verse 21. What do you see as the significance of verse 21 framing this discussion?

———————————————————————————

11. As a husband, what one step could you take toward fulfilling this picture of your role?

———————————————————————————

12. As a wife, how can you help your husband take this step?

Pray for a clear understanding and practice of how God intends husbands to treat their wives. Allow time for confession.

Now or Later

Look for examples of a husband loving unselfishly. Compare ideas. Did you recognize the same behavior or different ones? Did the wife feel loved in the way her husband intended or did she miss the message?

6

God's Design for Parents & Children

Teenagers say they are in trouble because their parents are selfish and don't care about them or listen to them. Parents say their teenagers are in trouble because they don't listen, and they want to have everything their own way. Whatever the reasons, many families are sharply divided because parents and children can't get along.

GROUP DISCUSSION. As you were growing up, what were your most satisfying experiences with your parents?

PERSONAL REFLECTION. Reflect on God's goodness in creating families for our good. Thank him for your parents and extended family, though no one has perfect parents. If you are a parent, thank him for your children, naming specific things that you appreciate about each one. Ask the Holy Spirit to teach you what you need to learn from this study.

Husbands and wives who find happiness by following God's principle of mutual submission discover that the same principle relates to bringing up children. Ephesians 6:1-4 reveals that neither parents nor children should be dominated by the other. *Read Ephesians 6:1-4.*

1. Paul continues to explain the meaning of "submit to one another out of reverence for Christ" (Ephesians 5:21). What effect would it have on parents and children if they submitted to one another in order to please Christ?

---

2. You may have grown up with a win-lose atmosphere in every family conflict. What difference would mutual submission have made in your struggles to mature?

---

3. Why is God's basic command to children: "Obey your parents" (vv. 1-3)?

---

4. The command to "honor your father and mother" is part of God's Ten Commandments. In Genesis 2:24 we saw that a man should leave his father and mother and cleave to his wife. How can we continue to honor our parents after leaving home?

---

5. Why is the first command to fathers something they should *not* do?

---

6. What attitudes and actions of parents exasperate children?

How can parents teach children to obey without exasperating them?

---

7. Instead of exasperating their children fathers are to "bring them up in the training and instruction of the Lord" (v. 4). What are the differences between training and instruction?

---

8. Children need *training* in things like honesty, respecting other's property, respecting authority, making choices, taking responsibility. In what practical ways can a parent give training in these areas?

---

9. In what different ways can parents *instruct* their children?

In what areas or topics do you (or would you) most want to instruct your children?

---

10. What are some ways you have learned (from your experience or from observing others) to manage the demands that training and instruction put on parents' time, attention and patience?

Praise God for the beauty and satisfaction of family life. Ask him to protect families from misunderstandings, conflicts and breakdowns.

Now or Later

If you are a parent: This week plan with your spouse one specific way you can obey God's commands to you in this passage.

If you are not a parent: Decide on one specific way you can express honor to your parents this week and do it.

7

God's Design for Sex in Marriage

1 Corinthians 7:1-11

Blaring messages about sex invade our daily lives—thanks to the media. In a culture where moral values are often ignored, it can be difficult to view sex as part of God's good creation.

GROUP DISCUSSION. Think about what you see and hear in music, magazines, TV and conversations. What messages about sex are you getting?

PERSONAL REFLECTION. Reflect on the fact that God declared everything that he had made, including sex, to be *very good* (Genesis 1:31). Ask God to help you to appreciate the beauty and joy of sex as he designed it—for your good.

The Corinthians lived in a sex-saturated society. Their city was notorious for the immorality associated with the temple of Aphrodite, goddess of love. They had written Paul with some questions. Should Christians completely abstain from sex? Was abstinence the answer to immorality? Paul answers their questions by giving guidelines for the healthy role of sex in marriage. *Read 1 Corinthians 7:1-11.*

---

1. In response to the immorality around them the Corinthians wrote to ask whether it is good for Christians to be married. What are the main points of Paul's answer?

_____

2. The apostle gives the same standards and principles about sex to both husbands and wives. How does this compare to our culture's ideas or to what you thought the Bible taught?

_____

3. What are the responsibilities and benefits of the sexual relationship for both husbands and wives (vv. 2-4)?

Why may either spouse initiate sex?

_____

4. Why do you think that Paul emphasizes responsibilities of husbands and wives rather than their rights?

_____

5. Why might a couple refrain from sexual intercourse (v. 5)?

What cautions does Paul give to those who do refrain?

6. How does this passage speak against using sex as a reward, or withholding sex as punishment for one's spouse?

---

7. Why are marriage and singleness both acceptable to God (vv. 7-9)?

---

8. In a fallen world, conflicts and barriers do come between spouses. Paul recognizes the temptation to separate. What options are open to the couple having marital problems (vv. 10-11)?

How might discussing their problems with a mature Christian couple or counselor promote reconciliation and prevent separation?

---

9. In studies 4 and 5 we looked at the principle of mutual submission in Ephesians 5:21. How are the principles of sexual responsibilities given here a practical application of mutual submission?

Pray that Christians will have God-given strength and wisdom to practice sex in marriage that honors the Lord and meets their needs.

Now or Later

This week make a date with your spouse to discuss your joys and/or frustrations about your sexual relationship. Reflect on how our culture's emphasis on achieving maximum sexual pleasure affects your ability to talk about your legitimate sexual needs.

8

God's Design Protected

Matthew 5:27-30

"I wasn't looking for sex when Frank and I first became friends. It was just so good to talk to a man who was thoughtful of my feelings. We could talk so easily. He made me feel good about myself. Dave hadn't listened to anything I said in months." This is a common beginning to the story of a destroyed marriage.

GROUP DISCUSSION. We can think of rules as limiting our freedom or as serving to protect us. Think of a rule your parents made that you thought was unnecessary but you now see was really for your protection. What changed your thinking?

PERSONAL REFLECTION. Reflect on your struggle with sin and the sexual temptations around you. Talk to God about your desire to be pure in his sight.

God's design for a permanent, exclusive, one flesh relationship is under constant attack. In Matthew 5 Jesus reinforces God's protection of his design and the seriousness of sin. *Read Matthew 5:27-30.*

1. How does Jesus' attitude toward adultery differ from our culture's attitude?

---

2. What kinds of behavior are prohibited by the command "Do not commit adultery"?

---

3. People usually give reasons for their adultery: "We love each other," "I don't love my wife anymore," "My spouse doesn't meet my needs." Why are there no exceptions given to the command against adultery?

---

4. Jesus' definition of adultery includes lustful looks and thoughts (v. 28). We can't prevent evil thoughts from coming to our minds, but we do choose what we do with them. What is the difference in being tempted by a lustful thought and committing adultery in our hearts?

---

5. What is the difference between lust and God-given sexual desires?

---

6. In what ways are the eye and hand avenues to sexual temptation (vv. 29-30)?

---

7. Obviously, gouging out an eye or cutting off a hand would not remove our ability to lust. How does Jesus intend us to apply his commands in verses 29-30?

---

8. How might the way we dress, our conversation and our lifestyle be a source of temptation to someone of the opposite sex?

---

9. How does Jesus' teaching here make flirting or trying to make a spouse jealous off limits?

---

10. How can a couple protect their marriage against a third person who flirts with or pursues one of them?

---

11. How does God's command for faithfulness in marriage show his loving concern for our highest good?

Pray for the intention to avoid adultery or anything leading up to it. Confess your sins. Ask God for courage and faith to stand against culture's acceptance of adultery.

Now or Later

Make a list of the qualities that first attracted you to your spouse. Then make a date with your spouse this week so you can read your lists to each other. Express appreciation for every positive contribution your spouse has made to you.

9

God's Design for Conflict

Ephesians 4:25-32

Watching an ice hockey game, you see two distinctive patterns of play. Some players use their skating and puck-handling skills to finesse their way through the defensive line. They avoid conflict as much as possible. But others seem to relish conflict. In fact, they go out of their way to flatten their opponents.

In the early days of a marriage, people often try to dodge conflict as much as possible. We paper over our differences and pretend we're not hurt by disagreements. But eventually we lose control and a fight erupts.

GROUP DISCUSSION. When you were growing up, how did your parents handle conflicts and anger?

PERSONAL REFLECTION. Ask God to help you understand your initial responses to conflict. Pray for the Holy Spirit to empower you to obey what you learn in this study.

The Bible doesn't gloss over the fact that people have differences. The way of success is not to ignore the problem or to fight the other person but to work out our conflicts with mutual love and respect. In Ephesians 4 we find ways to handle conflicts constructively. *Read Ephesians 4:25-32.*

1. What common ways of handling conflict does this passage condemn?

2. In verse 25 we are told to "put off falsehood and speak truthfully" because we are members of one body. What subtle forms of lying or not speaking the truth take place between husbands and wives?

3. How is it possible to be angry and not sin (vv. 26-27)?

4. Recall a time when you felt very angry. Would you have been more likely to say, "I am angry," than to say, "You make me angry"? Which is more accurate and why?

5. What is the connection between how long we are angry and the likelihood of sinning?

6. In a conflict how would the instruction in verse 29 protect your relationship as you work out your differences?

7. Since the command not to grieve the Spirit is placed here (v. 30), what kinds of behavior must grieve the Spirit?

8. The apostle Paul dramatically contrasts the two ways to handle conflict (vv. 31-32). How would the positive attitudes and actions cancel out each of the destructive behaviors in verse 31?

_____

9. How do you feel when your spouse or a friend treats you in the ways described in verse 32?

_____

10. How does verse 32 answer the argument that some hurts are too terrible to forgive?

_____

11. Marital conflicts generally focus on money, rearing children, sex, in-laws and how to divide the work load. How could the principles in this passage change the way you handle one of the conflicts in your family?

Confess unresolved conflicts to the Lord. Ask for the peace and wisdom of Christ to rule in your hearts.

Now or Later

Decide to work on one area of marital conflict. In the coming week consciously apply the principles from this study to this problem area. If you are studying in a group, pray for each other. If you are studying on your own, ask another couple you trust to pray for you.

10

God's Design for Handling Money

After his return from a visit to Europe an early Chinese philosopher declared, "The European god is not so large as the Chinese. It is small, so small that one can take it in the hand. It is sound, made of silver and gold, bears weapons and inscriptions, and is called money."

GROUP DISCUSSION. Money represents different things to different people: control, status, security, freedom, pleasure and so on. What did you learn about the meaning of money from your parents? Do you agree or disagree with them? Explain.

PERSONAL REFLECTION. Recall times you have been anxious about money. Recall ways God provided for your material needs. Talk to God about your feelings toward what you have or wish you had. Ask him to help you develop a godly attitude toward money and the way you use it.

Money and possessions can tyrannize a marriage and wreck a relationship. That's why the Bible makes repeated demands on our attitude toward and use of money. We must be liberated from the idol of money if we are to achieve God's best in our marriages. Paul's counsel to Timothy can help us come to grips with the issues. *Read 1 Timothy 6:6-10.*

---

1. How do contented people and those who want to get rich differ in their attitudes toward money?

---

2. Think about someone whom you see as a contented, godly person. How would you describe the "great gain" that has come to that person (v. 1)?

---

3. God speaks against laziness (Proverbs 24:30-34) and against neglecting one's family (1 Timothy 5:8). How are laziness and neglect different from being content with what you have?

---

4. People have basic *needs* for food, clothing and shelter. But society creates many additional *wants* in our minds. How can godly people learn to be content when their needs are met?

---

5. Credit cards, installment buying and impulse buying can be traps that lead to ruin for an individual or a marriage. How can you avoid these traps?

6. How does this passage warn against making money your goal (vv. 9-10)?

_____

7. What limits are you willing to put on your standard of living to have time with your family and to give to those in need?

_____

8. *Read 1 Timothy 6:17-19.* Why would the rich need the three commands in verse 17?

_____

9. God richly provides us with everything for our enjoyment according to verse 17. What does it mean to you to live in light of this fact?

_____

10. How can we become "wealthy" in the way God desires (v. 18)?

How can a regular savings plan be part of obeying these commands?

_____

11. What present and future benefits will result from our right attitudes toward and use of money (v. 19)?

12. How is this perspective on the eternal significance of money truly counter-cultural (vv. 17-19)?

Pray for wisdom, courage and faith as you earn, save, give away and spend your money.

Now or Later

We must learn to manage money or it will manage us. Choose the assignment that best suits your needs.

1. To learn how you are spending money, keep a complete record of every penny spent for two weeks. Use a notebook to write down every expenditure as it is made. Then evaluate your spending habits. Decide what changes you need to make.

2. Buy a budget book at a stationery store. Make a budget. Discuss each item with your spouse. After two months, evaluate the budget. Decide what changes you need to make.

3. Recall one of the disagreements you and your spouse have had over money. How would an attitude of contentment, a right perspective on the value of money, a sense of security in God and an understanding of the responsibility to share your money change anything you said in the disagreement? Discuss this issue with your spouse this week in the light of this study.

11

God's Design for Love

1 Corinthians 13

Love is used to sell everything from soda pop to automobiles. Unfortunately some people love their spouses the way they love a new car. When they get too many miles on them, they trade them in on a newer model!

GROUP DISCUSSION. Take a vote. Do you think (1) love is a feeling; (2) love is a choice; (3) love is both? Discuss why you voted as you did.

PERSONAL REFLECTION. Think about the people who have truly loved you. Reflect on times when you have felt God's love most personally. Thank God for his love to you in Jesus and through others.

The fleeting, sentimental, Hollywood version of "I love you," bears no resemblance to God's definition. Although poets and authors have written volumes about love, none can compare with what the apostle Paul wrote in 1 Corinthians. *Read 1 Corinthians 13.*

---

1. How does Paul's description of love compare with your vote about love in the opening discussion?

2. Apparently it is possible to do sacrificial religious service without love. How does Paul evaluate such activity (vv. 1-3)?

3. How would a lack of love for your spouse cancel the value of your sacrificial service in the church or other Christian activity?

4. It is possible to busy yourself with service or Christian activities to avoid solving a conflict with a family member. How can you handle this temptation?

5. What impresses you about the list of what love is and is not (vv. 4-7)? Why?

6. How is our focus different when we are patient and kind instead of envious or boastful?

7. How do rudeness, self-seeking and being easily angered show an absence of love?

8. Marriage counselors warn against keeping accounts of wrongs because of the destructive power of such lists. How would the positive actions of love in verses 5-7 protect you from this danger?

9. "Love is giving someone the benefit of the doubt." How well does this summarize verse 7?

10. The Corinthian Christians boasted about their gifts of prophecy, tongues and knowledge, which are all temporary. How do the illustrations of the child and the mirror show what they should have been more concerned about (vv. 8-13)?

11. What helps you to measure whether you are really more concerned about faith, hope and love—things that remain—than about things that pass away?

12. In these studies you have discovered and examined the values and principles of God's design for a lasting, exclusive, satisfying marriage. Why would a regular review of 1 Corinthians 13 encourage you in living by that design?

Thank God for his love in Christ and for the beauty and power of Christian love. Pray for integrity and joy in your love relationship.

Now or Later

Identify any childish characteristics you need to replace. Identify any you think your spouse should replace. This week make a date to share your answers with each other. Listen well. Each one should repeat what the spouse said in a way acceptable to him or her. Pray for each other. Set a time next week to discuss your progress and struggles.

Leader's Notes

Leading a Bible discussion can be an enjoyable and rewarding experience. But it can also be *scary*—especially if you've never done it before. If this is your feeling, you're in good company. When God asked Moses to lead the Israelites out of Egypt, he replied, "O Lord, please send someone else to do it!" (Ex 4:13). It was the same with Solomon, Jeremiah and Timothy, but God helped these people in spite of their weaknesses, and he will help you as well.

You don't need to be an expert on the Bible or a trained teacher to lead a Bible discussion. The idea behind these inductive studies is that the leader guides group members to discover for themselves what the Bible has to say. This method of learning will allow group members to remember much more of what is said than a lecture would.

These studies are designed to be led easily. As a matter of fact, the flow of questions through the passage from observation to interpretation to application is so natural that you may feel that the studies lead themselves. This study guide is also flexible. You can use it with a variety of groups—student, professional, neighborhood or church groups. Each study takes forty-five to sixty minutes in a group setting.

There are some important facts to know about group dynamics and encouraging discussion. The suggestions listed below should enable you to effectively and enjoyably fulfill your role as leader.

Preparing for the Study

1. Ask God to help you understand and apply the passage in your own life. Unless this happens, you will not be prepared to lead others. Pray too for the various members of the group. Ask God to open your hearts to the message of his Word and motivate you to action.

2. Read the introduction to the entire guide to get an overview of the entire book and the issues which will be explored.

3. As you begin each study, read and reread the assigned Bible passage to familiarize yourself with it.

4. This study guide is based on the New International Version of the Bible. It will help you and the group if you use this translation as the basis for your study and discussion.

5. Carefully work through each question in the study. Spend time in meditation and reflection as you consider how to respond.

6. Write your thoughts and responses in the space provided in the study guide. This will help you to express your understanding of the passage clearly.

7. It might help to have a Bible dictionary handy. Use it to look up any unfamiliar words, names or places. (For additional help on how to study a passage, see chapter five of *How to Lead a LifeBuilder Bible Study,* IVP, 2018.)

8. Consider how you can apply the Scripture to your life. Remember that the group will follow your lead in responding to the studies. They will not go any deeper than you do.

9. Once you have finished your own study of the passage, familiarize yourself with the leader's notes for the study you are leading. These are designed to help you in several ways. First, they tell you the purpose the study guide author had in mind when writing the study. Take time to think through how the study questions work together to accomplish that purpose. Second, the notes provide you with additional background information or suggestions on group dynamics for various questions. This information can be useful when people have difficulty understanding or answering a question. Third, the leader's notes can alert you to potential problems you may encounter during the study.

10. If you wish to remind yourself of anything mentioned in the leader's notes, make a note to yourself below that question in the study.

Leading the Study

1. Begin the study on time. Open with prayer, asking God to help the group to understand and apply the passage.

2. Be sure that everyone in your group has a study guide. Encourage the group to prepare beforehand for each discussion by reading the introduction to the guide and by working through the questions in the study.

3. At the beginning of your first time together, explain that these studies are meant to be discussions, not lectures. Encourage the members of the group to participate. However, do not put pressure on those who may be hesitant to speak during the first few sessions. You may want to suggest the following guidelines to your group.

☐ Stick to the topic being discussed.

☐ Your responses should be based on the verses which are the focus of the discussion and not on outside authorities such as commentaries or speakers.

☐ These studies focus on a particular passage of Scripture. Only rarely should you refer to other portions of the Bible. This allows for everyone to participate in in-depth study on equal ground.

☐ Anything said in the group is considered confidential and will not be discussed outside the group unless specific permission is given to do so.

☐ We will listen attentively to each other and provide time for each person present to talk.

☐ We will pray for each other.

4. Have a group member read the introduction at the beginning of the discussion.

5. Every session begins with a group discussion question. The question or activity is meant to be used before the passage is read. The question introduces the theme of the study and encourages group members to begin to open up. Encourage as many members as possible to participate and be ready to get the discussion going with your own response.

This section is designed to reveal where our thoughts or feelings need to be transformed by Scripture. That is why it is especially important not to read the passage before the discussion question is asked. The passage will tend to color the honest reactions people would otherwise give because they are, of course, supposed to think the way the Bible does.

You may want to supplement the group discussion question with an icebreaker to help people to get comfortable. See the community section of the *Small Group Starter Kit* (IVP, 1995) for more ideas.

You also might want to use the personal reflection question with your group. Either allow a time of silence for people to respond individually or discuss it together.

6. Have a group member (or members if the passage is long) read aloud the passage to be studied. Then give people several minutes to read the passage again silently so that they can take it all in.

7. Question 1 will generally be an overview question designed to briefly survey the passage. Encourage the group to briefly survey the passage, but try to avoid getting sidetracked by questions or issues that will be addressed later in the study.

8. As you ask the questions, keep in mind that they are designed to be used just as they are written. You may simply read them aloud. Or you may prefer to express them in your own words.

There may be times when it is appropriate to deviate from the study guide. For example, a question may have already been answered. If so, move on to the next question. Or someone may raise an important question not covered in the guide. Take time to discuss it, but try to keep the group from going off on tangents.

9. Avoid answering your own questions. If necessary, repeat or rephrase them until they are clearly understood. Or point out something you read in the leader's notes to clarify the context or meaning. An eager group quickly becomes passive and silent if they think the leader will do most of the talking.

10. Don't be afraid of silence. People may need time to think about the question before formulating their answers.

11. Don't be content with just one answer. Ask, "What do the rest of you think?" or "Anything else?" until several people have given answers to the question.

12. Acknowledge all contributions. Try to be affirming whenever possible. Never reject an answer. If it is clearly off-base, ask, "Which verse led you to that conclusion?" or again, "What do the rest of you think?"

13. Don't expect every answer to be addressed to you, even though this will probably happen at first. As group members become more at ease, they will begin to truly interact with each other. This is one sign of healthy discussion.

14. Don't be afraid of controversy. It can be very stimulating. If you don't resolve an issue completely, don't be frustrated. Move on and keep it in mind for later. A subsequent study may solve the problem.

15. Periodically summarize what the group has said about the passage. This helps to draw together the various ideas mentioned and gives continuity to the study. But don't preach.

16. At the end of the Bible discussion you may want to allow group

members a time of quiet to work on an idea under "Now or Later." Then discuss what you experienced. Or you may want to encourage group members to work on these ideas between meetings. Give an opportunity during the session to allow people to talk about what they are learning.

17. Conclude your time together with conversational prayer, adapting the prayer suggestion at the end of the study to your group. Ask for God's help in following through on the commitments you've made.

18. End on time.

Many more suggestions and helps are found in *How to Lead a LifeBuilder Bible Study*.

Components of Small Groups

A healthy small group should do more than study the Bible. There are four components to consider as you structure your time together.

Nurture. Small groups help us to grow in our knowledge and love of God. Bible study is the key to making this happen and is the foundation of your small group.

Community. Small groups are a great place to develop deep friendships with other Christians. Allow time for informal interaction before and after each study. Plan activities and games that will help you to get to know each other. Spend time having fun together-going on a picnic or cooking dinner together.

Worship and prayer. Your study will be enhanced by spending time praising God together in prayer or song. Pray for each other's needs—and keep track of how God is answering prayer in your group. Ask God to help you to apply what you are learning in your study.

Outreach. Reaching out to others can be a practical way of applying what you are learning, and it will keep your group from becoming self-focused. Host a series of evangelistic discussions for your friends or neighbors. Clean up the yard of an elderly friend. Serve at a soup kitchen together, or spend a day working on a Habitat house.

Many more suggestions and helps in each of these areas are found in the *Small Group Starter Kit*. You will also find information on building a small group. Reading through the starter kit will be worth your time.

Study 1. God's Design for Marriage. Genesis 1:26—2:25.

Purpose: To learn God's purpose and plan for creating marriage.

Question 1. Avoid a possible tangent of arguing whether a characteristic is purely male or female. Tenderness is usually associated with females and forcefulness with males, but both can be found in one person. Look for what the characteristic tells us about God's image and how we need both types of characteristics to fully understand God's image. Such characteristics as being creative; having mind, emotion, will, freedom of choice; the need to love and be loved; and so on are human and not gender related.

Question 2. Some people may be struggling with accepting their gender or sexuality. Knowing that sexuality is part of God's good creation may help to free them.

Question 3. Be sure to include responsibilities in 1:26, 28; 2:15-17 and resources in 1:28-30; 2:8, 9.

Question 4. You might ask the group to visualize the scene and Adam's emotions as the parade (and time) go by.

Question 6. Encourage some to express Adam's feelings with voice reflection and words of their own.

Question 7. Notice what is taught about the priorities, permanence and exclusiveness of marriage. You may want to build a bridge between 2:23 and 24. Notice the phrase *for this reason.* What reason is given in 2:23? Males and females are made of the same stuff. She is God's answer to the man's loneliness.

Question 8. Couples may need to discuss how to prevent a baby from separating them. How can they take time for each other with the pressure of children's needs?

If appropriate to the needs of the group, you may want to point out that God designed marriage to be between male and female. There is no place for homosexual marriage in God's plan.

Question 9. Their nakedness was both literal and symbolic. The almost universal desire of fallen people is to cover their bodies, at least partly. See Genesis 3:7.

Question 11. Since this is your first study together, some may feel shy about speaking to this question. Acknowledge that fact and allow for thoughtful silence. Accept every response. Encourage honesty, not just saying what people think they should say. The group will benefit from openness.

Now or Later. Encourage couples to use the "Now and Later" portions for discussion at home between studies.

Study 2. God's Design Marred. Genesis 3.

Purpose: To see the source of the broken relationships between husband and wife.

Question 1. In *Effective Bible Teaching* Jim Wilhoit and Leland Ryken say when we are studying a story, "We need to be active as participants or spectators of the action. . . . Before we interpret its meaning we need to relive it. We need to be active in visualizing, in imagining scenes, in entering into the spirit of events, in identifying with characters" ([Grand Rapids, Mich.: Baker, 1988], pp. 210-11).

As the group names the conflicts, keep asking if there are other conflicts until they are is satisfied that they have identified all of them.

Question 2. It might be helpful to identify ways Satan uses the same tactics today.

Question 6. God treats them as responsible creatures by allowing them to suffer the consequences of their choices. Questions enable them to accept responsibility or assign blame.

Question 7. Think of what they enjoyed before their disobedience and what they lost.

Question 9. Be prepared to share one experience if no one else does. The group will follow your lead.

Question 10. Avoid the tangent of the role of pain in natural childbirth. Focus on the change in their relationship before and after sin. "To love and to cherish becomes 'To desire and to dominate.' While even pagan marriage can rise far above this, the pull of sin is always towards it" (Derek Kidner, *Genesis*, IVP, 1967 (reprinted 2008), p. 76).

Question 11. It is important to keep God's character front and center in this story. Allow ample time to think through the big picture.

Study 3. God's Design Restored. Galatians 5:13-26.

Purpose: To discover that the Spirit brings freedom from sinful patterns in marriage. In the Spirit, husbands and wives are free to enjoy the beautiful oneness of God's original design.

Question 3. Ask for specific illustrations if people are open.

Question 5. We can assign a very different motive to an act than what the person intended. Learning to talk about what our spouse means by any action is most important. Learning to talk about what we think it means is also important.

Question 6. While the group will probably not need to have an in-depth knowledge of the background to verses 16, 18 and 25, the following may be of interest and help you as the leader.

Verse 16 can be translated, "So I say; *keep on living* by the Spirit," since Paul assumes the Galatians are already living that way. The verb translated "live" in verse 16 refers to our conduct or *manner* of life. It is different from the word *live* in verse 25, which refers to the *source* of our life.

The word translated "led" (v. 18) is used of a farmer herding cattle, a shepherd leading sheep, soldiers escorting a prisoner to court or prison, and of wind driving a ship. It does not refer to guidance but rather to being led toward holiness.

The word translated "keep in step" (v. 25) means to walk in line or be in line with. (See John Stott, *The Message of Galatians*, The Bible Speaks Today [IVP, 1992], pp. 152-53.)

Encourage each other to think very specifically and practically about what these commands mean.

Question 9. If needed, recall some illustrations from the Bible or from God's work in your life that demonstrate God's love, joy; peace, patience, kindness, goodness and so on.

Question 10. Tell some stories of your own about marriages that you admire and respect.

Question 11. Talk about decisions couples have to make: what to do, spending money; use of leisure time, relations with in-laws, work and professional demands, commitments to church, and so on.

Study 4. God's Design for Wives. Ephesians 5:21-33.

Purpose: To understand the principle of mutual submission as a basis for all other relationships. To explore Paul's instructions to the wife.

General note. As you approach this study; be aware that members of your group may have strong feelings about this passage and topic. They may have heard teaching on submission in the past that they found painful or offensive. And couples may have differences of opinion as to how this passage as lived out. Encourage everyone that no matter what their perspective is on the passage, there is something each of us can gain from studying it. Submitting our will to our spouse's will is an essential part of living as a married couple.

Question 2. Unfortunately mutual submission is often overlooked in popular discussions about the roles of wives and husbands. Therefore it is important to flesh out this basic command before talking about specific duties.

Question 3. You may need to give an example to help the group recognize mutual submission. Someone may describe a situation that could have been improved or avoided if mutual submission had been practiced.

Question 4. As Christians we submit to the Lord with respect, trust and love, as to One who cares for our best interests—although sometimes we submit reluctantly.

Question 5. Show how Scripture emphasizes that our mutual commitment to Christ's lordship is the basis for satisfying human relationships. If both partners are not committed to Christ, serious problems arise. This is why Paul enjoined Christians not to marry unbelievers (2 Cor 6:14).

Question 6. This question uses *us* rather than *the church* to personalize the discussion.

Question 7. There are examples in Acts 6:1-6; 9:10-19; 10:9-22; 11:27-30. Read these in your preparation. Use the illustrations most helpful to you.

Question 8. "In everything" (v. 24) refers to the marriage relation specifically. It does not, for example, include the wife's political views or her choices in home decorating.

Questions 9-10. Help the group to be specific about the ways they think about their spouses. Do they dwell on the positives and what attracted them to each other, or on their differences? Have they learned to give each other the benefit of the doubt? Do they pray for each other? Do they speak to each other respectfully and warmly?

Study 5. God's Design for Husbands. Ephesians 5:21-33.

Purpose: To understand how God wants a husband to treat his wife.

Question 1. Encourage short, specific responses. Avoid tangents. This is not the time for general discussion. Following questions will bring out the details.

Question 2. Be sure the group observes the differences in the commands. Later questions will explore the meaning of each one. Here the group may want to discuss the impact of three comparisons. The high standard set for the husband's love may seem overwhelming.

Questions 3-4. Christ wants the church's highest good, her growth, development, purity. Christ has high goals for the church and lovingly helps her meet them. The husband might consider what kind of goals he has for his wife. Does he think of his wife's need for reaching her full potential or only of her meeting his needs?

A husband may need to remind himself of who and what he is in Christ, so his self-image is accurate. If he feels defensive, threatened by his wife's growth, life will be harder for both of them. You may need to ask the group to think about how a husband's self-image affects his caring for his wife.

Question 5. If we realize how much time and effort we spend on caring for ourselves (eating, grooming, exercising, shopping, recreating and so on), we feel the thrust of the command to husbands.

Question 6. Encourage the group to think of specific ways Jesus cares for the physical, emotional and spiritual welfare of the church. If it is not mentioned in the discussion, point out that Jesus' loves unconditionally. He continues to love no matter how the Christian behaves. The husband is not released from his duty if his wife doesn't please him 100 percent all the time. Like Jesus, he is till to keep caring for her highest good.

Question 7. If someone has joined the group who wasn't in study 1, you might review, or ask someone else in the group to review, the main ideas from your discussion of Genesis 2:24. Be brief.

Question 8. The note on unconditional love in question 6 needs to be applied to both wives and husbands. Encourage honest discussion of our temptation to return evil for evil rather than returning good for evil.

Question 9. Help the group to consider our tendency to think first about "what I get out of it," rather than to think first about our responsibility.

Questions 11-12. Allow time for personal reflection. Perhaps some will not want to speak to this practical application. By this time, however, people should be encouraged to do so.

Study 6. God's Design for Parents & Children. Ephesians 6:1-4.

Purpose: To learn that mutual submission is the context for the parent-child relationship. To understand the responsibilities of parents and children to each other.

For further reading. *Guilt Free Parenting* byRobert and Debra Bruce, Ellen W. Oldace (Dimensions for Living, 1997); *How to Really Love Your Child* by Ross Campbell (Inspirational Press, 1992); *Honey For A Child's Heart* by Gladys Hunt (Zondervan, 1989). *Hide or Seek* by James Dobson (Revell, 1979); *The Two Sides of Love* by Gary Smalley and John Trent (Pocket Books, 1992).

Question 1. Paul gives the principle of mutual submission (5:21) as an introduction to the instructions to husbands and wives, parents and children, and masters and slaves. Parents fulfilling their responsibility to Christ won't manipulate their children, and children won't divide and control their parents.

Question 2. Typically we all like to win. Show how this is contrary to mutual submission. Ask for stories that will show either the damage of win-lose conflicts or the growth from practicing mutual submission. Be careful so the stories do not degenerate into either self-pity or nasty criticism.

Question 3. Someone may ask, If my parents aren't Christians, am I to obey them? The phrase "in the Lord" helps us to see that obeying our parents is part of our obedience to Christ. If a parent were to commit an immoral act or something in violation of God's clear commands, it becomes an issue of obeying God rather than man (Acts 4:19-20).

Note that children are told to obey both parents. You might ask how parents can agree on what they require of their children and how they can work out requirements both of them can live with.

Question 4. If the group raises the issue of the parents not deserving respect in the eyes of their children, note that the Bible requires honor of parents and of government, not because the person or authority is perfect but because of their position (Exodus 20:12; Romans 13:1-2; 1 Peter 2:13-14, 17).

Questions 5-6. Encourage honest discussion of how parents' behavior can discourage, anger or promote rebellion in a child.

Questions 7-10. The definitions of training and instruction should help the group to explore activities beyond simply lecturing. You might use the example of what training means in athletics and the military.

You may want to discuss how children can be properly trained when both parents work and the children are under someone else's care. The high value God gives to child rearing contrasts with the value some elements in our culture give to it.

Now or Later. Ask the members of the group to choose the appropriate assignment and be prepared to report briefly on their progress at the beginning of the next meeting.

Study 7. God's Design for Sex in Marriage. 1 Corinthians 7:1-11.

Purpose: To understand sexual responsibilities in marriage.

For further reading. For some in the group this subject may be loaded with misgivings, guilt or fear. These books may be helpful: *Sexual Intimacy in Marriage* by William Cutrer and Sandra Ghaln (Kregel, 1998); *Seven Lies About Sex* by Alice Fryling (InterVarsity Press, 1997); *Singles at the Crossroads* by Albert Y. Hsu (InterVarsity Press, 1998); *Restoring The Pleasure* by Clifford L. and Joyce J. Penner (Word, 1993).

Question 1. Perhaps some are studying this passage for the first time. They might be surprised by Paul's frankness. Be prepared for some awkward moments. Have the summary of Paul's main points clearly in mind so that none of them are overlooked.

Question 2. Try to draw out as many real-life examples as you can. Give time for some misconceptions to surface. Keep in mind that some may have failed in previous relationships and are seeking forgiveness and acceptance.

Questions 3-5. Individuals differ in their sexual needs. One spouse may need sex more frequently. Studies show that the male's highest point of sexual activity is during late teens and early twenties. The female's highest point typically comes at about thirty. How would the principles in this passage help spouses to work out their differences in a loving, understanding manner?

One partner may be dissatisfied sexually but not communicate this to the other. "If he (or she) loved me, he'd know what I need" is often used as an excuse for not talking about differences. You may want to ask the group how this passage presupposes that spouses are expressing their needs honestly to each other.

Question 6. All too often sex is withheld out of anger. When relations sour, it is inappropriate and self-defeating to use sex as a weapon to get one's own way. Meeting each other's highest needs is more important and more satisfying than playing tit-for-tat with sexual relations.

Question 7. In some circles singleness is frowned on as abnormal or second class. For others, marriage is viewed as the perfectly happy state. It may benefit the group to explore why both of these views are exposed here as myths.

Question 8. This is not the place to discuss whether or not divorce is biblical. Other Scriptural texts come into play on this subject. Encourage the group to stick to the main point: working for reconciliation rather than giving up on the marriage.

Some marriage problems are so common that almost every couple would have some experience handling them. If problems are faced early, solutions are easier to achieve. The group may need to discuss their attitudes toward seeking help from Christian friends and professionals.

Question 9. Help the group to think about the basic issue: my rights and my needs come first in sex. That is the typical view most of us grow up with. Give time for reflection on how radical biblical principles are. Mutual submission means yielding one's sexual rights for the sake of my partner's good, but also recognizing my partner's needs when "I don't feel like it."

Now or Later. Singles: what basic concepts about sex did you learn from your parents or observe in their relationship? For example, did they view sex as something to be enjoyed, tolerated, feared or avoided? How does the Bible affirm or contradict those concepts?

Study 8. God's Design Protected. Matthew 5:27-30.

Purpose: To understand the benefits of God's demand for faithfulness in marriage.

Question 1. Everyone will agree that adultery is no longer frowned on in society. But the stark commands of Jesus may shock some people. Do not take much time to berate society's ills in this regard. Spend more time talking about what Jesus said.

Question 2. Help the group to think about responsibilities and privileges in marriage that belong exclusively to our spouses and are not to be shared with anyone else (flirting, fondling, intimate conversation and confidences, and so on).

Questions 4-5. The issue is the difference between temptation and sin.

Jesus was tempted but without sin, so they are not the same. (See Lk 4:1-13 and Heb 4:15). People often worry and take on guilt for impure thoughts. When this becomes oppressive, we need to ask the Holy Spirit to guard our minds and to refrain from reading and watching things that inspire such thoughts.

Question 7. These commands give heightened caution to the dangers of sexual temptation through watching and touching. No one expected them to be carried out literally. There is no record of anyone having done so. Therefore Jesus' intention was to place a high wall of protection against the inroads of sin via our eyes and hands.

Question 8. Encourage honest discussion of how dress and behavior have encouraged impure thoughts. How have jokes, touching or other actions been a source of temptations?

Question 11. Remember God's original design in Genesis 1 and 2 was for a permanent, exclusive relationship which would meet our deepest needs. Any behaviors or attitudes that destroy our intimate oneness is not for our good.

Now or Later. If you are single, think of the qualities you need to build a permanent, exclusive, one-flesh marriage. Consider the qualities you would want your spouse to have. Talk with a Christian couple whose marriage you admire about your expectations.

Study 9. God's Design for Conflict. Ephesians 4:25-32.

Purpose: To learn to acknowledge and constructively deal with anger and conflict in marriage.

For further reading. *The Anger Workbook* by Les Carter and Frank Minirth (Thomas Nelson, 1993); *Love's Tug of War: Partnership Beyond the Power Struggle* by C. and J. Congo (Revell, 1997).

Question 1. Be sure the group brings out the basic differences between ungodly ways of dealing with conflicts and the biblical way. Perhaps some have come to accept their ungodly habits are irremediable. The biblical way may seem unrealistic and impractical to them.

Question 2. The group may need to discuss the role of silence. Can silence be a form of lying? Can silence be a dodge of the responsibility to speak the truth in love? Encourage the group to think of times when pretense, false impressions and refusing to admit one's feelings have sent a false message to their spouse.

Question 3. It may help to remember when Jesus was angry without sinning (Mk 3:5; Jn 2:13-17). One helpful paraphrase of Ephesians 4:26 is: "If you are angry, be sure that it is not out of wounded pride or bad temper" (J. B. Phillips).

Question 4. "I" statements about our feelings, wishes, needs and hopes are more accurate than statements about the other person's motives or actions. God holds us responsible for our actions and reactions. We can't blame someone else for our responses.

Question 5. Unfortunately, if anger is unresolved and is allowed to fester, it often turns into a grudge or, even worse, hatred.

Question 6. Talk about how words that build up one another often defuse anger. Ask for some examples of how this has helped avoid an angry conflict in some relationship. Be specific about examples of "grace" words.

Question 7. The issue is the Spirit's close identification with the Christian. He is grieved when one in whom he lives is verbally abused.

Question 8. Ask for illustrations of how kindness and compassion can prevent slander, bitterness and so on.

Question 9. Be ready to lead the way with an illustration of how you have felt when someone forgave you or treated you more kindly than you deserved.

Question 10. The standard of our forgiveness is that of God himself. In Christ he forgave the worst of sinners. Allow time for those who perhaps are carrying deep wounds from people they have not yet forgiven. Talk about the full meaning of God's grace.

Now or Later. Begin the next study with brief reports of your progress and struggles.

Study 10. God's Design for Handling Money. 1 Timothy 6:6-10, 17-19.

Purpose: To discover the godly attitude toward and uses of money, and to apply these principles to money management.

For further reading. *Breaking Out of the Plastic Prison* by James D. Dean and Charles W. Morris (Revell, 1997); *5 Steps to Successful Money Management* by Lee E. Davis (Broadman, 1993); *Living on Less and Liking It More* by Maxine Hancock (Victor, 1994).

Jesus said a great deal about money. He recognized its potential to control us through worry or greed. He stressed that money and possessions are never to be the source of our hope and security. You may want to familiarize yourself with some of what Jesus taught. See Matthew 6:24-33; Mark 10:23-31; 12:41-44; Luke 16:10-15.

Group discussion. Money is one of the three most common causes of marital conflict. Understanding how one differs from one's spouse in money decisions can defuse conflicts. The patterns we saw while growing up influence our attitudes toward money—how to earn it, save it and spend it, who pays the bills, individual checking accounts, and so on. Usually one partner spends more freely than the other. Working out spending habits that both can live with is what each couple must learn. Talking about our parents' use of and attitudes toward money can begin to give us the needed insights.

Question 1. By comparison with the rest of the world, Americans are rich. One definition of poverty is that the poor have no options. Encourage the group to think realistically about themselves.

Question 2. If the group has difficulty identifying the benefits of being content, ask them to think of someone they consider to be a contented person. What characterizes that person? What is attractive and admirable about her or him?

Questions 4-5. Our society is success oriented. Often success is measured by money, the things money can buy and the status that accompanies wealth. We are subtly pressured on every hand to accept society's values. These questions can help the group to recognize social pressures for what they are. The biblical value of being content goes counter to our selfishness and our culture.

Questions 6-7. Money itself is not the root of all evil, but the love of money is. Ask the group for specific ways people are trapped and destroyed by eagerness for money and what it can buy.

Question 9. If we see God as the one who provides all our needs, we can live free of worry and greed. In eagerness to be content we may be surprised at God's abundant provisions to those who trust him. Since God gives everything to be enjoyed, we don't need to feel guilty for the comfort and beauty God gives to us.

Question 10. The idea of earning money in order to be able to give it away will be a new idea to some. There is no clearer test of the power of money over us than our attitude toward giving. A regular savings plan provides for our family's needs as they arise, accrues interest and enables us to continue giving.

Questions 11-12. Paul's perspective reflects what Jesus taught. By being good stewards of what God entrusts to us, we demonstrate our trustworthiness to be given greater responsibilities.

Now or Later. Ask each one to choose one of the three assignments now. Next week begin with a report on any benefits or frustrations.

Study 11. God's Design for Love. 1 Corinthians 13.

Purpose: To understand God's standard and definition of love.

For further reading. *A Handbook for Engaged Couples* by Alice and Robert Fryling (IVP, revised edition, 1996), *A Handbook for Married Couples* by Alice and Robert Fryling (IVP, 1984), and *Fit to Be Tied* by Bill and Lynne Hybels (Zondervan, 1991).

Question 1. If love is just a feeling, then the marriage may be considered over when we don't feel loving toward our spouses. Note that Paul identifies love as actions and attitudes to be practiced. Feelings follow actions; they don't determine actions.

Question 3. Help the group to see that this is not an either-or situation. Obviously God is pleased with our service to him and the church. The main point is our motivation and what our service may do to our marriage. Love must inspire and motivate our service. It must also reign in our marriages.

Question 4. Avoiding problems is the issue. One can appear to be spiritual by a great deal of religious activity but use it to cover up a problem at home. This is not the same as each spouse having some time apart for meaningful activities.

Questions 5-7. Encourage specific examples of each characteristic. If one is missed, you might ask about that particular quality.

Question 10. Apparently Paul saw a serious inconsistency in what the Corinthians prided themselves on. He said they were puffed up with pride (1 Cor 5:2; 8:1) but lacking in love. We need to recognize our need to grow in love as evidence of our spiritual maturity. Help the group to see the priority of growing up in love.

Questions 11-12. If we concentrate on love rather than on our achievements, status and competition, we have something that lasts in old age and in eternity. Ask the group to be specific and practical about how to measure their values and priorities.

God's design honors him and enriches us when we focus on what is most important in our relationship. 1 Corinthians 13 must be read together and privately to help us keep the right perspective. Otherwise we so easily drift into the world's way of thinking about love and marriage.

Now or Later. If you are single, identify any childish characteristics you need to replace. Choose a friend, perhaps someone in the study group, with whom you can share your list. Listen well to each other. Repeat what the other says in a way acceptable to both of you. Pray for each other. Set a time next week to discuss your progress and struggles.

James W. Reapsome (d. 2017) served as editor of Evangelical Missions Quarterly *and the* World Pulse *newsletter. He was the author of LifeBuilder studies such as* Exodus, Hebrews, Grief, *and* Marriage. *Martha Reapsome is retired and living in Downers Grove, IL. Formerly she served as midwest director of Neighborhood Bible Studies, Inc., now known as Q Place, Dobbs Ferry, NY.*